981
B

Bennett, Olivia.

25300

A family in Brazil.

A Family in Brazil

LIBRARY OF CONGRESS CATALOGING-IN-PUBLICATION DATA

Bennet, Olivia.
  A family in Brazil.

  Originally published under title: Brazilian family.
  Summary: Describes the life of a twelve-year-old Brazilian
girl and her family, residents of the southern town of São Marcos.
  1. São Marcos (Brazil)—Social life and customs—Juvenile
literature. 2. Family—Brazil—São Marcos—Juvenile literature.
3. Brazil, South—Social life and customs—Juvenile literature.
[1. Brazil—Social life and customs] I. Taylor, Liba, ill. II. Title.
F2651.S175B46 1986   981'.21   85-23919
ISBN 0-8225-1665-9 (lib. bdg.)

Manufactured in the United States of America

3   4   5   5   6   7   8   9   10   96   95   94   93   92   91

A Family in Brazil

Olivia Bennett

Photographs by Liba Taylor

Lerner Publications Company · Minneapolis

Eliane Leonardelli is 12 years old. She lives in Brazil, which is the largest South American country, in the town of São Marcos (SAUW MAR- kus).

Her father is a truck driver and is away all week. He comes home on Saturday to spend the weekend with his family.

When Mr. Leonardelli comes home, Eliane's family rushes out to meet him. Eliane is the youngest in her family. Her brother and sister are named Eliseu and Elisete.

Buenos Aires

Montevideo

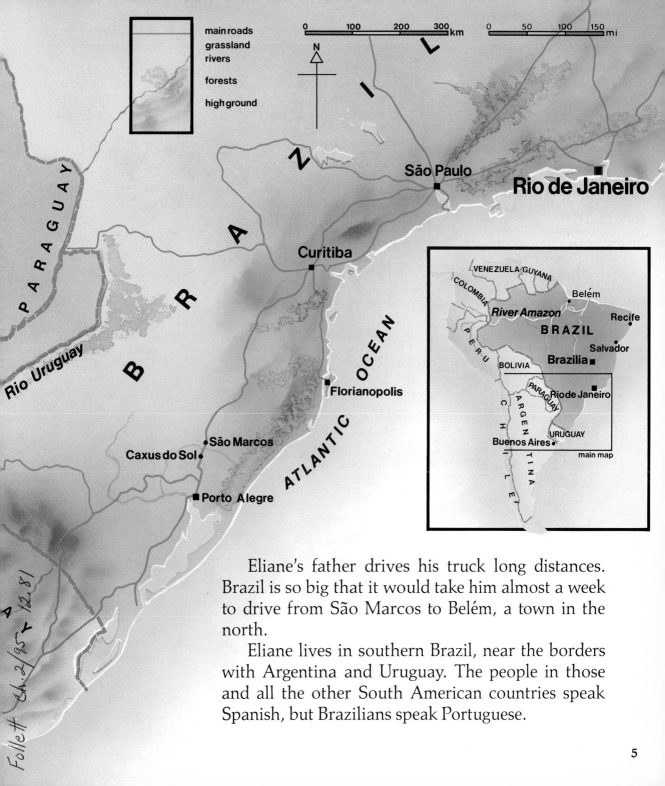

Eliane's father drives his truck long distances. Brazil is so big that it would take him almost a week to drive from São Marcos to Belém, a town in the north.

Eliane lives in southern Brazil, near the borders with Argentina and Uruguay. The people in those and all the other South American countries speak Spanish, but Brazilians speak Portuguese.

When Eliane's family has caught up on news with her father after his trip, Eliane cleans up the truck. Mr. Leonardelli bought the truck a few years ago.

Since her father usually gets home on Saturday and leaves again on Monday, Eliane's favorite day is Sunday.

On Sunday morning Eliane's father relaxes with a cup of green tea, called *mate* (mah-TAY). It is made from the leaves of a tree and looks like ground-up grass.

Mate is drunk through a special metal straw which has a small filter at the end to strain out the bits of leaf. Eliane thinks mate is too bitter, but lots of people in southern Brazil drink it. Her father loves it.

The best part of her family's Sundays is their *churrascou* (shuh-RASS-kew), or barbecue. Eliane helps her mother and Elisete make salad while her father and Eliseu light the charcoal.

The barbecue grill is in a small, open room on the side of the Leonardellis' house. Eliane knows many other families with barbecue rooms. It means they can have churrascou all year round, even in the rainy season in the summer. Winter in Brazil is from May to September.

After Eliane's father lights the fire, he sprinkles a piece of beef with lots of salt and cuts it into big chunks. He puts the beef onto long skewers, like thin swords, to go on the fire.

Then he makes a drink called *caiparinha* (kay-per-REEN-ya). It is made of crushed limes, ice, sugar, and home-made rum, and the glass is passed from person to person until it's empty. Eliane is allowed a sip, too. As soon as the glass is empty, Mr. Leonardelli makes some more.

Eliane tries a taste of the beef and the home-made pork sausages. Then everyone sits down to eat. The meat is sliced right onto their plates.

Churrascou is especially popular in southern Brazil because there are many cattle ranches in the area and people eat lots of meat. Most towns and cities have restaurants called *churrascarias*.

On Sunday afternoon, Mr. Leonardelli and Eliseu often watch soccer on television. They are fans of a team called Gremio (GREM-ee-oh) from Porto Alegre. Whenever Gremio wins an important game, people let off firecrackers all over town.

Sometimes, Eliane's father has to go away for more than a week. If he isn't home by Sunday, the family might go to a village *festa*, or celebration, to make up for missing their own churrascou.

Like most people in Brazil, Eliane's family is Catholic. Every Sunday, at least one of the local churches celebrates a special Mass or a saint's day, and everyone joins in a big churrascou afterwards. Sometimes hundreds of pieces of meat are barbecued in one afternoon.

At the village festa, Eliane will see some *gauchos* (GOW-chose) in cowboy hats with their baggy pants tucked into their boots. They are Brazil's cowboys. They herd cattle on the *pampas* (PAMpas), the grasslands which stretch south of São Marcos.

Eliane thinks her family is lucky because her father is usually home on Sunday. Some of her friends' fathers drive trucks to towns in the north, and are away from home for a month at a time. There aren't many railroads in Brazil, so most goods are moved by truck.

São Marcos is on one of the main truck routes in Brazil. Many people have jobs washing, fixing, or servicing trucks. There is a factory in town which makes parts for trucks.

Every October, at the Festa dos Motoristas, the truck drivers decorate their cabs and drive slowly past the church. The priest blesses them and sprinkles holy water on each truck.

Eliane lives in the same block as her mother's parents, three of her uncles and aunts, and eight of her cousins. Many families live very close to one another in São Marcos. Eliane thinks it is because so many of the fathers drive trucks and are often away from home.

Eliane's grandparents, the Fochezattos, bought the land ten years ago. One by one, the rest of the family has built houses there. Eliane's mother has eight sisters and they all live nearby.

Eliane's relatives all help each other. Her grandfather Fochezatto looked after Rico, Eliane's parrot, while her family was away on vacation. Eliane likes to talk to her grandfather. He knows all about the history of her family. His parents came from Italy, like many other people in southern Brazil.

Brazilians include a mixture of people. Indians lived there first. In the sixteenth century, Portuguese explorers and settlers began to arrive. Later, people came from all over the world, mainly Europe and Africa. Many of the Europeans settled in southern Brazil. In the north, more of the people from Africa settled.

Mr. Fochezatto has always lived near São Marcos. He says it has changed a lot since he was a boy. He used to be a farmer, like his father and brothers. But all his sons-in-law have jobs in factories or drive trucks.

São Marcos is growing fast. Many tall apartment buildings and several factories have been built. Eight of the factories make and bottle wine.

Most Brazilian wine is made in the area around São Marcos. Eliane's father often carries wine from São Marcos on his truck.

Eliane has heard that it was the Italians who started growing grapes and making wine in Brazil. Most of the grapes are grown on small farms and then taken to a wine depot. There the grapes are crushed and put into tall wooden vats to ferment and turn into wine.

At the depot, there is a machine which washes wine bottles, fills them with wine, and puts the corks in. The bottles go on a conveyor belt past a man who puts on the labels. Then Elaine's father and other drivers load the bottles onto their trucks, about 2,000 each trip.

The wine bottles and their plastic covers are made in São Marcos. One of Eliane's uncles is in charge of the glass factory. It is hot, smelly, and very noisy in the factory.

Outside the factory building is a huge, slippery, shiny pile of broken bottles. The pieces of glass are cleaned and separated from any trash. Then a man shovels the broken glass into a blazing furnace. The heat melts all the pieces into a glowing red, gluey mass of liquid glass.

The melted glass is used to make new bottles. The finished bottles are different shades of green, yellow, or brown, depending on the color of the old ones which went into the furnace.

Eliseu works in the plastic factory where the bottle covers are made. He is fifteen and this is his first job. He works from six P.M. until two in the morning.

He runs a machine which melts down little balls of plastic and molds them into bottle covers. The plastic covers are taken to the glass factory and fitted onto the bottles. Then the bottles are taken to the wine depot, to be filled with wine and end up on Mr. Leonardelli's truck.

Mrs. Leonardelli works at home, like most of Eliane's friends' mothers and older sisters. Mrs. Leonardelli weaves chair seats for the local furniture factory. Elisete and Eliane earn a little money by helping her.

A man from the factory comes to Eliane's house a couple of times a week. He collects and pays for the chairs that are finished and leaves thirty new, wooden chair frames behind.

When Eliane first started weaving with her mother, the work hurt her hands, but they are tougher now. The Leonardellis can do about twelve chairs in a morning, but they aren't very well paid.

The Leonardellis work on the chairs in a big room called a *porão* (por-ROW). The porão is also used to store firewood, herbs for making tea, homemade salami, onions, cheese, wine, soap, and anything else they want to keep safe and dry.

Eliane's house is built on a slope. The porão is the room underneath, which opens onto a sort of patio. All of Eliane's friends' houses are built this way.

Eliane goes to school in São Marcos. Her summer vacation is from January until the end of March. During vacation she earns extra money by babysitting. Her grandmother, Mrs. Fochezatto, likes to spend the afternoon with Eliane and the baby.

Mrs. Fochezatto washes clothes every week with soap she has made from pig fat. Eliane's family uses this kind of soap, too. They keep one or two pigs a year and make salami, sausages and soap from them. They keep the pigs in a pen at the end of the yard.

Eliane's family keeps some chickens and rabbits, too. They get some of the animals from her other grandmother, Mrs. Leonardelli. She has a farm with cows and pigs. Her farm is only a twenty minute drive from São Marcos, and Eliane loves visiting her on weekends.

Grandmother Leonardelli also grows some of the grapes which are made into the local wine.

Two of Eliane's uncles live on the farm with Grandmother Leonardelli, and all her other children are nearby as well. Her husband, Eliane's grandfather, died a few years ago, so there is a lot to do on the farm. Summer is a very busy time and a couple of cousins come to help her. Eliane helps pack ripe grapes into wooden boxes.

Mrs. Leonardelli grows figs, too. She makes them into jars and jars of delicious jam. She boils and stirs the figs in a copper pan for four hours. The jam bubbles and boils, and sometimes plops over the side. Mrs. Leonardelli keeps well away by using a spoon with an extra-long handle.

Grandmother Leonardelli always gives Eliane something to bring home from the farm. Eliane likes to eat her grandmother's delicious fig jam with bread and coffee.

In Eliane's house, the television is usually on. They get four channels, and there are programs most of the day. In the picture, Eliane's family is watching the Carnival parades in Recife and Salvador, two cities in the north of Brazil.

Carnival is the biggest and most exciting festival of the year in Brazil. It lasts for four days before the beginning of Lent. People dress up in costumes, dance in the streets, and celebrate day and night. There are parades, and contests for the best dancing and costumes.

Nobody works during Carnival, and in the big cities, like Rio, many stores and offices close. The further north in Brazil, the more people seem to celebrate Carnival. Much of the music and dancing comes from the songs and dances brought by Africans when they settled in Brazil.

In São Marcos, at the children's Carnival party, Eliane and her friends dress up and paint their faces. They dance nonstop for about four hours. Eliane's mother usually helps at the party, but last year she and Eliane's father went to Rio for Carnival.

Every year, Eliane's parents go on one trip together. Mr. Leonardelli says that other parts of Brazil are very different from São Marcos.

He's been to big, modern cities like Brasilia, the capital of Brazil. But he's also seen deserts, mountains, jungles and sandy beaches. Eliane has been on a few trips with him, but never further than São Paulo.

When Eliane's parents go away together, her grandmother Fochezatto or one of the aunts looks after her and Eliseu and Elisete. Eliane likes living next to her relatives. They share things they need and there's always someone to play with.

Most Saturday evenings, they go to church together. One very special thing Eliane's relatives share is a statue of the Virgin Mary. They pass it from one family to another each afternoon. When Eliane's grandmother has it she keeps it in her sitting room.

Brazilians call the Virgin Mary "*Nossa Senhora,*" which means "Our Lady." When Eliane and her mother shop in São Marcos, they usually go to the chapel dedicated to Nossa Senhora. They say a prayer and light a candle in her honor. The chapel is cool and very peaceful after the busy supermarket. Eliane likes to look at the new apartment buildings in São Marcos. But she prefers to live the way her family does, in their own house with a big yard, and family all around.

The Amazon River Basin

The Amazon River in northern Brazil is the second longest river in the world. Only the Nile River in Africa is longer. Oceangoing ships can travel on the Amazon's entire length within Brazil. Rain which falls on the river basin as far west as the Andes in Peru or Colombia drains into the Atlantic through the Amazon River.

The river basin is mostly lowlands covered with lush jungle and rain forest. An amazing variety of plants—over 3,000 different kinds of trees have been found in one square mile—make up the jungle. Howling monkeys, jaguars, colorful parrots, and anacondas (snakes) up to 30 feet long live in the forest.

Only about 7 percent of Brazil's people live in the Amazon region. It is as remote to most Brazilians as it is to any foreigner. The jungle has made it very difficult for Brazil to explore the area and use its resources.

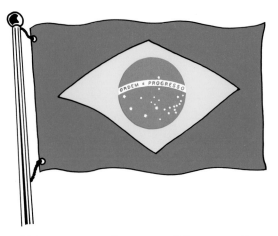

Facts about Brazil

Capital: Brasilia

Language: Portuguese

Form of Money: the cruzeiro

Area: 3,286,487 square miles (8,511,965 square kilometers)

    Brazil is slightly larger in area than the continental United States.

Population: about 153 million people.

    The population of Brazil is about half the population of the United States. It ranks as the world's sixth largest nation in population.

NORTH
AMERICA

Brazil

SOUTH
AMERICA

EUROPE

ASIA

AFRICA

AUSTRALIA

Families the World Over

Some children in foreign countries live like you do. Others live very differently. In these books, you can meet children from all over the world. You'll learn about their games and schools, their families and friends, and what it's like to grow up in a faraway land.

Lerner Publications Company, 241 First Avenue North, Minneapolis, Minnesota 55401